T0195789

OTHER PUBLICATIONS (pending)
By Dr. L. D. WHYTE

The natural approach to the management of arthritis
The natural approach to the management of diabetes
The natural approach to the management of asthma
The natural approach to the management of obesity
The natural approach to the management of cancer
The natural approach to the management of immune
    deficiency disorders
The natural approach to the management of sexual
dysfunction
Nutrition the natural way
Healing modalities
What is your body saying to you?
Detoxification
Mental flossing
Vaccines - fact or fiction
Laughter is the best medicine

PERFECT HEALTH IS UNQUESTIONABLY *YOURS*

Dr. L. Danovan Whyte

BALBOA.PRESS

A DIVISION OF HAY HOUSE

Balboa Press books may be ordered through booksellers or by contacting:

Balboa Press
A Division of Hay House
1663 Liberty Drive
Bloomington, IN 47403
www.balboapress.com
1 (877) 407-4847

Print information available on the last page.

All Scripture quotations are taken from the King James Version.

ISBN: 978-1-9822-4105-6 (sc)
ISBN: 978-1-9822-4106-3 (e)

Balboa Press rev. date: 01/10/2020

Perfect health is your divine birthright.

Choose it or lose it

… .The choice dear friend is

Unquestionably yours

- DR. L. D. WHYTE

THIS BOOK IS DEDICATED TO ALL SEEKERS OF TRUTH AND SELF-EMPOWERMENT.

My intention is to question our belief system and to seek the truth in all our affairs. The truth in health is the focus of this publication.

MY PEOPLE …. YOU SHALL KNOW THE TRUTH AND THE TRUTH SHALL MAKE YOU FREE.

John 8:32(KJV)

In memory of my grandmother, Mrs. Katie McKenzie

Who taught me all about health, by being a perfect example.

CONTENTS

INTRODUCTION

As a trained physician I entered the profession with enthusiasm and zeal. This was fuelled by a burning desire to make a difference, in alleviating sickness, suffering and disease. Soon my belief in the power of medical science to cure illnesses became shattered, as there was precious little we could truly claim to cure....... Unbelievable? Think about it, after so many years of scientific medicine what have we cured? Diabetes? arthritis? High blood pressure? cancer? We are however, very good at suppressing the symptoms or removing the tumours, never once addressing the reason for their existence.

It was my inability to identify what we cured, that resulted in my journey becoming one of seeking truth in health at all cost. I was compelled to re-evaluate everything I was taught and held to be factual. Subjecting them to unbiased scrutiny, in an effort to find the truth in matters of health and disease.

In pursuit of the truth, my paradigm shift was guided by the question - "What if the body was not making an error, but in fact doing what it was supposed to do?" That is the fundamental question I set out to answer in the following pages.

I thank God for the guidance, truth, wisdom and ever-present love I have received in compiling this volume.

This publication is long overdue, as I have often wondered whether we were really ready and willing to take control of ourselves. Taking responsibility for ourselves and be courageous enough to accept the truth about ourselves or simply be content to follow blindly as we are told.

This book summarises my own growth and development. It represents my determination to seek the truth in all things regardless of the consequences.

I questioned the fact that those who could access the best that the health industry offered, were often not as healthy as the seemingly 'poor uneducated' person who could not. In fact some of the healthiest persons I have met, have had minimum or no exposure to the health industry. Proof of the adage… 'God takes care of 'fools' and babies'.

Those who could afford the services offered by the health industry were often doomed to a life of popping one pill after the other or a chain of surgical procedures. One way or the other they were tied to the system in order to 'survive'.

This is so because the multiplicity of pills and medicines were not effecting cures. They were only relieving symptoms or exchanging one symptom for another.

The arthritic patient, for example, gets good relief from the painkillers, but there is scant regard for the damage being done to the stomach, liver or kidneys, by the medication taken. After all, if and when these systems begin to show evidence of malfunction, there are other medicines that are usually given to suppress them as well.

Treating the side effects of the treatment and the side effects of their side effects, is now the order of the day. Patients will continue to visit doctors for the same or even different complaints and the doctor becomes an indispensable pill pusher....'a successful practitioner.'

But what of the patients' success? Who cares? Once they can gain access to the medication or other medical services geared at relieving the symptoms.... "No problem". They have health insurance anyway or if not, then they should.

Such an approach leads to the conclusion that we have all collectively agreed to a theory of self-deception, a theory that convinces us that our healing lies in the hands of others and not ourselves.

The great 'god' of science therefore becomes our saviour, and we prostrate ourselves as we marvel at its wonders. We become completely oblivious to the greatest marvel of all...our divine perfect selves made in the image and likeness of our Creator; absolutely capable of self-healing. A healing that would appear if only we would stop blocking the process and allow our perfect health to be expressed.

We would come to the realization that perfect health is the natural way of life and blocking its natural manifestation, due to errors in our thinking, results in disease. The true role of a physician in such a situation therefore, is that of a teacher and coach in matters of physical, emotional and spiritual health. A "hollow bone," - a channel or conduit, through which Gods healing energy may be directed to effect healing. Our scant regard for the spiritual and emotional side, is evident by their conspicuous absence from the doctors training curriculum. We have been led to a level of self-deception where physicians are viewed as demi-gods with absolute control of the physical body (errors in thinking).

Hence the physician's role, in the modern era has been relegated to one of amusing the patients with gadgetry, and terminology designed to confuse the unwary, while nature is discouraged from taking its course.

I implore you to read with an open mind and without fear. *"You shall know the truth and the truth shall make you free"* *St. John 8:32.(kjv)*

Free from sickness, lack, limitation and fear

IF WE ALL ARE THINKING THE SAME THING,
THEN NONE OF US ARE THINKING.

DON'T LET THEM FOOL YOU OR EVEN TRY TO SCHOOL YOU, YOU HAVE GOT A MIND OF YOUR OWN, SO GO TO HELL IF WHAT YOU ARE THINKING IS NOT RIGHT. LOVE WILL NEVER LEAVE US ALONE, FOR OUT OF THE DARKNESS THERE MUST COME OUT THE LIGHT........ BOB MARLEY

THE BASIS OF DISEASE

Friendly or good bacteria live in harmony with the body under normal conditions of health. These bacteria serve a wonderful function in enhancing growth, tissue repair and other vital life functions, promoting our natural good health.

However, under the influence of adverse condition e.g. impurity, toxicity and acidification, good bacteria will merge and/ or mutate (change) in order to ensure their continued existence.

This process of mutation results in the formation and progression of microbial life forms. These microbes follow a pleomorphic (changeable) pattern resulting in greater pathogenicity (destructive or disease producing power) with each stage of development.

The process of change and adaptation of these smaller life forms, transforms them from being harmless and supportive to becoming dangerous and destructive in an effort to survive. In other words, under bad conditions, good microbes, example, bacteria will become bad bacteria.

Disease causing germs (microbes) will show an affinity for (be attracted to) weakened tissues and organ systems. This is because they grow fastest in the presence of weak devitalised or dead cells, degeneration, decay and putrefaction, developing rapidly in such conditions.

- The symptoms we display are dependent on the organ systems involved. For example, if the pancreas is being challenged by acid toxic damage and secondary microbial growth, then its ability to produce insulin would be compromised, resulting in poor blood sugar control or diabetes.
- The body will try to heal itself by eliminating toxic products, e.g. the by-products of microbial activity and toxins introduced to it.

This process of elimination is often misconstrued as the primary illness and, unfortunately suppressed e.g. diarrhoea, sinus drainage, and sputum.

Prevention and correction of disease may be achieved by reducing the body's exposure to toxicity - spiritual, mental and physical.

Illness is not a way of life but the result of a way of life...

- Dr. L. D. Whyte

ERRORS IN THINKING

The methods we employ to contaminate ourselves are often based on ignorance lack of awareness and errors in our thinking.

S elf
   I nflicted
      N onsense

Errors in thinking, <u>S</u>elf-<u>I</u>nflicted <u>N</u>onsense (SIN) results in decisions that disturb the normal harmonious function of our being. It is this production of non-harmonious frequencies/vibrations that results in dis-harmony and dis-ease.

The following are examples of error in thinking.

"I prefer processed foods because they are convenient and they do not spoil".

Truth...they cannot be better than the source from which they came. What are the possible effects of the preservatives (embalming agents) used, which are foreign to our bodies? Have you ever wondered why these foods cannot spoil? Simply because they are already spoilt, by the chemicals, dyes and the entire process of adulteration.

"Prosperity is only achieved through money"

No wonder money has become such an obsession, our ever-present focus, our prayer, our "new god". A new master means we have become enslaved and must therefore suffer the consequences. A sure recipe for stress and dis-ease

Happiness is conditional
When I have Ten million dollars,
When the children are grown,
When I find the perfect mate,
When my neighbour removes,
When I achieve.....

Then I shall be happy.

At this rate happiness will never be attained, but remain a fleeting illusion. Happiness comes from within and the only thing needed to be happy is to be.

Become aware of the 'eleventh commandment'

"Go thy way and be happy in this world"

This is the simplest way to change the world....change yourself by obeying this commandment.

"Go thy way and be happy in this world".

Dr. L. D.Whyte

Ignorance is our greatest impurity.

Dr. L. D. Whyte

Lifting your vibration

All life and matter have a specific oscillatory frequency, vibration or energy pattern by which it can be identified.

Pathogens - bacteria, fungus, etc. vibrate at lower frequencies than human tissue. Vibrant health exists whenever high frequencies far out-number low vibratory frequencies. Lifting ones vibratory level can therefore increase ones feeling of well-being.

This may be achieved by self-induction e.g., love, thanksgiving, forgiving, laughter, spinning, imagery, etc.

ONE SICKNESS ONE DISEASE

The effect of toxic impurities within the body is to create damage to susceptible tissues. Whenever this imbalance occurs then harmless microbes, example, good bacteria become modified to varying microbial forms in an effort to remove the damaged tissue and restore harmony. Hence, pathogenic (disease forming) microbial forms are to be found wherever there is damaged tissue.

Tissues may become susceptible as a result of inherent genetic weakness, or injury (physical toxins, emotional toxins,) the weakest systems are the first to become affected. Persons with a family history of diabetes, genetically have a compromised pancreas. Therefore, when exposed to toxic impurities, there is an increased likelihood for this system to be affected.

A damaged pancreas will show the behaviour corresponding to the derangement of its usual function, that is, inappropriate insulin production. Each individual is unique in genetic make up and life experience. It is unlikely that we would all have the same inherent weaknesses of our organ systems. This is the reason we do not all respond the same way to the same toxic insults. The resulting myriad (multiplicity) of disease profiles is just a representation of the varying methods of expressions of the one disease…. acid toxicity (impurities) and secondary mycotoxicosis (The poisonous effect of bacteria, virus, fungi etc.). It should be noted that even a genetically compromised system would function adequately, with the help of other supporting systems as long as the body's toxic load is kept to a minimum.

Inherent in all living things is the will to survive and heal itself. The body, therefore, is not making any errors in its functions. Often, it is only trying to undo the injuries we have inflicted on ourselves.

By the indiscriminate suppression of the body's responses in eliminating or correcting toxic insults, we in fact interfere or block the natural healing response. (See symptoms friend or foe)

Naturally the body facilitates the elimination of toxins through sweat, sinus drainage, sputum, periods, semen, nails, hair, gastric juices, tears, etc.

SYMPTOMS

FRIEND OR FOE

What are symptoms............? These nuisances that seem to come about when we least have the time to deal with them. They seem to disrupt our routine resulting in untold discomfort. Coughs, colds, diarrhoea, fever headaches, pain rashes etc. But what really are their functions?

So far the prevailing view is to regard them as illnesses and disease (malfunctions of the body), hence, we have developed a whole industry geared at eliminating or suppressing these maladies.

Cough suppressants, painkillers, anti-pyretics (ant-fever), anti-allergy and cold medicines etc.; certainly indicate that an all out war is being waged against our symptoms. We seem to regard them as punishment and do not pay much attention to their reason for existence.

Why should a sane intelligent body turn against itself and decide to punish itself?

Let us try to look at our symptoms differently; they may really be trying to teach us something. Try to trust the innate wisdom of your normally intelligent body. The one that is constantly carrying out actions like breathing, digestion, tissue repair, co-ordination, etc. without asking for our help.

Symptoms are often the body's response to what we have done to ourselves, and often times are simply methods of elimination or confinement of the toxic load we have been exposed to. In fact they are wonderful messengers often highlighting the errors we have made. But it is so much fun to kill the messenger …then we do not need to heed the message.

Diarrhoea

This method is frequently employed by the body to rid itself of toxic food products and infections. It results in rapid expulsion of faeces and is often very debilitating. The rapid fluid loss can lead to dehydration.

We have deemed this symptom as socially unacceptable and so our primary response is often to stop the process with absolutely no regard for its reason.

The message in this symptom is that we have exposed ourselves to some potentially toxic agents, which the body does not care to keep.

Our treatment however does the complete opposite because as we stop the process the toxins are forced to remain inside the body. A better response would be to increase your water intake in an effort to flush out and dilute the offending agent, while preventing possible dehydration. Coconut water is an excellent rehydrating agent. Abstaining from solid food also reduces the risk of worsening the condition. It is also advisable to locate the possible source of the toxic agents in order to learn the lesson and prevent a recurrence.

COLD, SINUSITIS AND COUGHING

If the body was unable to eradicate the toxic load through diarrhoea, then other methods may be used e.g. elimination via

the sinuses and the lung, cold, sinusitis, coughing, sore throat etc. may therefore result.

Unfortunately these symptoms are viewed with the same level of fear and trepidation, so once again we try our best to suppress them.

When these symptoms are suppressed, the toxins, along with the accumulated mucous, remain in the body, challenging the body to find yet another creative method of elimination. A reduction of the intake of mucous and mucous forming foods would significantly reduce the dependence on this method of elimination.

SKIN RASHES

The use of body fluid is always an excellent vehicle for the body to eliminate toxins. Failure to remove the toxins by the above methods may result in an attempted removal via sweat. Toxins coming out through sweat may result in damage to the skin in the form of rashes, abscesses, boils, eczemas and other skin irritations. The skin may also be responding to external toxic agents coming in contact with it. Again, knowledge of the source of toxicity would greatly assist in treating and preventing the condition.

Reminder - Toxins are most often of an acid nature and invariably result in tissue damage and destruction. This sets the stage for infections, parasites and other scavengers to proliferate. The repeated obstruction of the body's natural attempts of self-purification, as seen above, will result in an acid build up and subsequent infection overgrowth.

Fever

The increase in body temperature is often frightening and so there is a high demand for medicines to stop the fever. First, ask yourself "Why was the fever present?"

Whenever there is a significant overgrowth of infection the body responds with a fever.

The higher temperature makes it difficult for the growth and multiplication of the microbial forms and hence, assists the body's immune system in minimising the body's infection load. This may be considered as natural pasteurization.

The fever is an excellent messenger, telling us of the dire state of acidity and contamination of our bodies, hence encouraging the infections to grow.

Suppressing the fever alone therefore is not good enough. The underlying cause should always be addressed. Assisting the body would certainly remove the need for a fever, e.g. detoxifying the body and flushing out the toxins with water.

Fever is also a good indicator that the body is going through a change (transformation) in its toxicity level and hence its level of vibration.

Pain

Pain is undoubtedly our most feared symptom and the desire to stop pain regardless of the cause, is the order of the day. But why do we have pain?

Pain represents a blockage of energy flow and is in fact, the cry of tissues starved of energy. Pain is a powerful messenger telling us that something is wrong.

The interruption of energy flow may be due to a variety of causes from trauma to toxicity. Toxins may cause inflammation resulting in pain in sensitive areas. Also blockage to acupuncture meridian energy pathways may also result in pains.

Many excellent painkillers exist. The injudicious use of these agents without addressing the cause of the pain can have disastrous results. It is comparable to a motorist seeing the oil warning light and simply disconnects the light. …. He will soon be faced with the dire consequences of operating an engine without oil.

Vomiting

Vomiting is an extremely annoying symptom and many good agents are available to suppress it.

But why is the body doing this?

This is a method of expulsion of unwanted agents and of eliminating excess acids, another method of purification.

It follows therefore that the suppression of this symptom is not addressing the cause of the problem. The body is trying to purify itself of an acid overload so our best response may be to assist the body in removing the excess acid that has been accumulated.

Running away or suppressing our symptoms only delays the inevitable.

Symptoms (SINtoms), is the price we pay for errors in our thinking.

Paying back the devil so to speak.

The symptoms are wonderful messengers, but we need to stop killing them before getting the message.

RUNNING AND RUNNING AND RUNNING
AWAY...YOU CAN'T RUN AWAY FROM YOURSELF

........BOB MARLEY

THE EFFECTS OF SYMPTOM SUPPRESSION

In general the net result of suppressing our symptom is the retention of agents (impurities) within the body, which the body had good reason to eliminate.

Not being programmed for self-destruction, the body tries another clever method of self-preservation, under trying circumstances. This results in the storage of toxic impurities. This process has it's own complications.

Many storage methods are available e.g.

Fat cells, tumours (fibroids, prostate enlargement, breast lumps), stone formation (kidney, gallbladder), plaques (in blood vessels, cataracts) spurs, joint crystals (arthritis), cysts, etc.

With continued symptom suppression the body becomes increasingly toxic encouraging more infections to grow. This results in intense pressure on the immune system to keep these microbes in check, hence, the immune system becomes exhausted and incapable of coping with cancer cells and other degenerative diseases. The stage is now set for the proliferation of autoimmune and other immune deficiency disorders.

Symptoms are not the problem but they occur in an attempt to solve the problem

Dr. L. D. Whyte

SOURCES OF TOXICITY

Toxins are impurities, which are potentially injurious to the body, as they do not act in harmony with the body. They are usually of an acidic nature and often result in cell damage death and decay. The main sources of toxicity are foods, environmental factors and mental/spiritual toxicity.

FOOD TOXINS

Devitalized foods (dead foods) provide an environment in which infections and parasites thrive. These are foods without life energy, incapable of reproduction and growth.

All dead foods encourage the growth of infections and promote acidity within the body, setting the stage for sickness and disease. Remember that most disease forming germs are scavengers thriving on dead substances in an environment of decay, putrifaction, acidity and oxygen deficiency

EXAMPLES OF DEAD FOODS

SUGAR...the commercially prepared, extracted, devitalized product found in cakes, buns, sodas, biscuits, bread, etc.

DAIRY PRODUCTS.... Milk, cheese, butter, margarine, ice cream, condensed milk, skimmed milk, powdered milk etc.

MEAT PRODUCTS...All flesh breeds infection and corruption.

PROCESSED PRODUCTS.... Foods that are canned, preserved, dyed, genetically engineered, chemically treated irradiated.

REFINED FOODS...e.g. white rice and flour.

Dead foods are also mucus-forming adhering to the intestinal lining forming a nest for infections, parasites and worms. These parasites will then traverse the entire body to find suitable, susceptible and weakened areas to colonise. This results in the derangement of normal function of these areas.... Resulting in sickness and disease.

ENVIRONMENTAL TOXINS

We are all exposed to many toxic environmental products e.g. insecticides. Weedicides, air fresheners, smoke, radiation, cosmetics, industrial gasses and wastes, etc. Whatever we are exposed to, we are interacting with. If we interact with it then we are likely to absorb it. So if the product is acidic and toxic, then we are absorbing an acid toxic agent. Just remember that acid toxicity brings about tissue damage, death, decay and associated infection growth.

MENTAL TOXINS

Probably the most toxic agents to the body are the thoughts that we entertain. As we harbour thoughts of fear and doubt, we become anxious, depressed, tense and stressed out ....all of which are acid forming reactions. These feelings are usually fueled by our hate, anger, greed, unforgiveness, judgement, condemnation, criticism, envy, jealousy, shame pride, guilt, resentment, intolerance, impatience, self-righteousness etc. All these thoughts are based on our fears; so they all result in acid toxicity and its consequences, i.e. tissue damage, cell death, decay and disease.

Stop for a moment and contemplate the effect of each of these negative emotions on yourself as compared to those to whom they are directed.........Frightening isn't it?

It is said that resentment is like a burning coal that we hold in our hands with the intent of throwing it at the person we are resenting.........

Somebody is sure to get hurt ...guess who?

If you think you can or you cannot ...

you are right

HENRY FORD

DETOXIFICATION
(REVERSING THE PROCESS)

This is the process by which acid toxic impurities are assisted to exit the body.

It is a process that the body is carrying on all the time (see symptoms).

Fluids that are likely to leave the body (excretions) are the usual routes employed. Diarrhoea, cough, sputum, sinus drainage, sweat resulting in rashes, fever, tears, urine etc. These may be associated with fever, headaches, muscle and joint pains and flu-like symptoms.

In order to achieve detoxification, we must first reduce our intake and production of impurities (see sources of toxicity). The active elimination of existing toxins may be aided by the use of any of a number of simple natural products such as aloe vera (sinkle bible), castor oil, senna, noni (duppy soursop), cascara, sarsaparilla, etc.

Changing the diet to predominantly live whole foods e.g. fruits, vegetables, complex carbohydrates, nuts, grains, peas and beans, etc. aids in the cleansing and elimination process.

If the rate of elimination of toxins is increased then clearly the routes of elimination must become more active, hence, our symptoms seem to flare up…"We appear to get sicker".

By increasing our water intake, eight to twelve glasses of pure water per day, we dilute our toxins and speed up their elimination through the urine in preference to the other routes that are so uncomfortable.

The body produces new cells every second. These new cells are supposed to replace old damaged cells. But if the new cells are produced in the same old toxic environment then they will behave like the old cells.

By giving the new cells a chance to be themselves, that is to provide them with the newer, cleaner environment that they desire for proper functioning. Then they will do what they do best…promote healing.

'If yu wan good yu nose ha fi run' ......(Jamaican proverb)

Meaning

If you want good, you have to be prepared for the necessary sacrifice.

PRESERVING THE BLUEPRINT

The mind is ultimately responsible for what happens in the body. ...foods cannot be blamed. They certainly did not enter our body by chance but by our choices (based on what we believe about them). Many toxic agents came in because we invited them e.g. cigarette smoke, nicotine, alcohol, drugs, cosmetics insecticides, etc. Even the toxic thoughts we adhere to are reflecting our choices. Although the body also affects the mind, our reaction once again, is also a choice based on our belief system. The mind is therefore the ultimate blue print and architect of the body.

A mind engulfed in fear results in anxiety, depression, stress and tension. These reactions are acid forming and toxic to the self. Just become aware of the physical changes we go through when these thought patterns are entertained... churning in the stomach, increase in heart rate, breathing irregularity, lumps in the throat, etc

ALL BASED ON FEAR.

False
Evidence

Appearing
Real

Negative emotions are often used to justify our fears e.g. hate, anger, envy, jealousy, unforgiveness, guilt, shame, resentment, criticism, intolerance, impatience, judgement etc. They are all based on fear, promoting anxiety stress and tension and are therefore acid forming and toxic…**to the self.**

Fear basically is a reflection of ignorance, darkness and the absence of truth.

While **LOVE** represents knowledge truth and light.

We all fear the unknown as we imagine all the potential hazardous outcomes based on inadequate information… ignorance.

"I do not know what this is but suppose it could cause harm and then this harm may result in further complications, which may lead to further problems etc, etc." An assumption based on lack of knowledge (ignorance) is causing us to worry about future events, which are purely based on imagination….not facts.

We use the experiences of the past; project them as anxieties of the future and in the process sacrifice the present.

The solution would therefore be to learn to overcome fear with love.

But how can you love anything or anyone without first loving yourself? What we are displaying to our 'loved ones' is "what we think love is" until we truly love ourselves.

As stated earlier "love is about light, truth and knowledge", so we must first apply these principles to ourselves. To love yourself is to know yourself, be truthful to yourself and let your light shine (by removing our toxic impurities that act as a filter ... blocking the natural light that is within)

WHAT WE FEAR, IT IS DIFFICULT TO LOVE
BUT WHAT WE LOVE, WE CANNOT FEAR

So you think you already love yourself and this does not apply to you. Well here is a simple test to check if you really love yourself.

If you love yourself ...... **Would you poison yourself?**

Yet look at what you have been eating and exposing yourself to.

If you love yourself ....**would you hurt yourself? Would you carry so many burdens on your heads?**

Just reflect on your anxieties and attachments.

If you love yourself ......**Would you not be happy most of the time?**

"I have been down on the rock for so long I seem to wear a permanent screw"

Now do we really love ourselves or do we all have a lot of homework to do?

It is not easy to love the self, because we know too much about ourselves ......

'BE ANXIOUS ABOUT NOTHING'

Philippians 4:6 (kjv)

"I have been down on the rock for so long I seem to wear a permanent screw"

Bob Marley

We know what we are guilty of,
What we are ashamed of,
What we do not want others to know about us, etc.
So we hide behind masks and secretly burden ourselves
with these fears.

Ponder for a moment
    Aren't these burdens representing
    errors in our lives?
    At the time of making the error, did
    You know better?
    Were you acting out of knowledge
    (love) or ignorance (fear)?
    If you knew better would you have
    Done better?

These errors are our teachers either we learn from them
or we repeat the lesson.
Know yourself… Know the truth about yourself…… you
are **not** your mistakes

You are a wonderful child of the Universe who have made mistakes

You are a wonderful child of the Universe who have made mistakes
......so what?

I AND THE FATHER ARE ONE..john 10:38

It is very important to discontinue the process of labeling ourselves by our behaviour, especially our errors, e.g. Thieves, liars, cowards, etc. The process of seeing ourselves differently and recognising the truth about ourselves is called forgiveness.

Forgiving our self. This is a most important step in learning to love our self. You may not yet be ready to forgive your neighbour, but forgive your self for being unable to forgive him/her. Try it now; you will be amazed at how good it feels. Remove the burdens. This is an essential step in the healing process.

As we learn to love ourselves we will recognise that our neighbours are just like us, making their own errors and learning in the process, so now it becomes easier to .... "Forgive them for they know not what they do".

We are all making choices based on the limitations of our knowledge.

Love is the most important aspect of the healing process. It is the only human emotion that does not make the body acid. Being alkaline it neutralises the acid toxicity, creating the pure environment that is essential for healing.

The healing process, which is all about purification, is not complete until the purifying power of love is being expressed. No matter how well you eat or clean up the external environment if you cannot forgive your grandmother for writing you out of the will you are still toxic. Love purifies and keeps the blueprint clean setting the stage for a flawless end- product.

BE YE TRANSFORMED BY THE RENEWING OF YOUR MIND….romans12:2 (kjv)

Healing is purification and it comes from self-adjustment.

….Dr. L. D. Whyte

NATURAL APPROACH TO THE MANAGEMENT OF INFECTIONS

Definition

For purposes of this discussion I am taking the liberty of expanding the meaning of infections to include all microbial forms, which may from time to time live in our bodies. This definition would therefore include viruses, bacteria, fungi, parasites, both disease forming (pathogenic) and non-disease forming (non-pathogenic)

Viruses - are small organisms (smaller than bacteria), which tend to live by invading the cells of its host and taking over their role. They do not have a cell wall and have a single stranded RNA at the core. Viruses can only be seen through an electron microscope or a Rife microscope, not by an ordinary light microscope. Often they are associated with illnesses such as the common cold, measles, chicken pox, hepatitis, AIDS, herpes. Efforts to kill viruses with medication are often complicated by the fact that they become a part of the host cell and hence, killing them destroys the host cells.

Bacteria - are larger than viruses and hence, visible under an ordinary light microscope. They have a cell wall and are capable of living outside the host cells. At the core they contain two strands of RNA and are therefore referred to as DNA. Bacteria are often associated with illnesses such as abscesses, gonorrhoea, tuberculosis, and typhoid. Medication to kill bacteria is readily available.

Fungus - these are larger than bacteria and visible to the naked eye as branching overgrowths commonly called moulds. The green overgrowth seen on spoilt bread and cheese are due to fungal growths. They can grow inside and outside of the human body especially in cases of severe deficiency of the immune system. They are associated with diseases such as vaginal candidosis (candida), liver spots, dandruff, and thrush. Many researchers are convinced that they play a significant role in the growth of cancer. Anti-fungal agents are widely available.

Parasites - This group includes the larger life forms, which may live in our bodies e.g. worms. They can exist in any part of the body not just the intestines. The term infestation is more apt in describing these conditions, but they are being included here for purposes of completion in understanding the subject of infections. Illnesses such as debility, scabies and filaria may be associated with this group.

Where do they come from?

Infections may enter the body from external (outside) sources such as contaminated foods, air, water, sexual contact, etc. Several diseases are directly related to poor hygiene and are proof enough of this source of infection. Typhoid, cholera and dysentery are typical examples.

Sometimes infections appear without any obvious source of external contamination. Vaginal yeast infections in virgins, pneumocystis carnii in immuno-compromised persons, and fungal overgrowth after antibiotic treatment are typical examples.

Nature of infections - Why is it that a person who has not been having an infection, suddenly develop infections in an area that has been cut or bruised? It would seem as if infections are just lurking around, inside and outside the body waiting for the right conditions to grow. But just what are these conditions?

The presence of dead cells....tissue damage and destruction from injury of any type results in an increase of infectious activity. Infections are scavengers; they thrive on dead tissue or any condition that promotes death, decay degeneration, acidity and toxicity. Once the conditions are right, infections will continue to grow.

All conditions that lead to cell injury and death, i.e. physical e.g. trauma or chemical from toxic impurities (acid toxicity), will promote the growth of infectious forms. (See pathological basis of disease by this author). **NB**. Acid toxicity may arise from devitalised foods, exposure to toxic environmental substances and toxic thoughts.

Infections, like all life forms, will do whatever it takes to survive. Often this may involve mutation i.e. changing their form to adapt or conform to the prevailing environmental conditions.

Have you ever wondered why the same insect spray is not continuously effective against a population of insects or antibiotics against the same type of infection? We claim that they have built up resistance.

Yes, this is exactly what mutation is about ......the changes made by the organism to adjust itself to survive even under extreme conditions. It should be noted that the changes within the infections might result in newer forms, which have a different pattern of behaviour than the previous form. Hence the resulting disease pattern produced may be distinctly different from the pre-existing pattern.

This is why when we treat with antibiotics the original symptoms disappear only to be followed by another pattern of illness. We are quick to label this as a different illness......so again we continue to treat the side effects of the previous treatment.

It is interesting to note the rate at which these infections grow and multiply. The life cycle of infections is very short. ...seconds to hours, hence the speed with which we become contaminated by their presence.

The things we nourish will flourish

Dr. L. D. Whyte

They grow rapidly when the conditions are right and they die rapidly when the conditions are not favourable. Even under favourable conditions they do not die but de-evolve to the forms in which it existed previously. Ultimately, in a healthy environment, they regress to the state that we refer to as good bacteria. Here they coexist with the host in harmony and perfect health.

Beliefs

We are often of the opinion that infections are things that we catch from external sources only. We therefore become focused on killing the offending infections, believing that this is the solution to the problem.

What are the facts? Catching anything is not a passive action ….one does not catch a ball by doing nothing ….the hands have to be prepared to receive the ball. Infections can only grow in an environment that is receptive and conducive to their growth.

If a contagious infection is introduced into a room filled with people, not every one present will become infected. Why is this? Infections entering fertile soil will flourish and those meeting an unfavourable soil will not. Infections have been known to develop, e.g. vaginal candida and chlamydyia in virgins. Are these from external sources?

Antibiotics given to immune compromised patients are obviously useless in eliminating infections; otherwise these patients would not be so plagued by infections. Hence our dismal failure in treating AIDS cases.

Killing infections without changing the conditions that encouraged their growth is a waste of time and effort. Infections are like flies…regardless of how effectively we kill flies with insecticides, more will appear if the garbage that nurtured them remains. In fact after repeated use of the same insecticide, the flies will develop immunity to that particular agent. The newer generations have mutated (changed) in order to ensure their survival. As we compare the role of antibiotics in the killing of infections, we can see the similarity with the flies and insecticides. INFECTIONS WILL ALWAYS CHANGE WHEN THEIR SURVIVAL IS THREATENED BY ANY TOXIC AGENT.

Vaccination is the single most prevalent and most preventable cause of infant deaths

Dr. Viera Scheibnerova

Hence, we can now understand the need for newer and newer antibiotics... second, third and fourth generation antibiotics.

If we got rid of the garbage, would there be a need to kill flies?

If we cleaned up our bodies, would there be a need to kill infections? (remember that they thrive on dead substances and acid toxic conditions).

WE HAVE WAGED A WAR AGAINST **INFECTIONS** **but we are clearly losing. We must therefore change our methods.**

VACCINES

What about vaccines? Is this the solution to the infection problem?

This technique is based on the theory that if the body is exposed to an infection then it will force the immune system (defence mechanism) to respond. Resulting in an improved capacity to fight off any future challenge by this same germ.

In an effort to reduce the ill effects of this procedure, the germ being inoculated is usually altered to diminish its ability to cause disease. In some cases the inoculating germ is killed and in others the live germ is modified to reduce its pathogenicity (disease causing potential).

A lot of fantastic claims have been made about the benefits of this procedure and its responsibility in eradicating some diseases. However, there are also claims that some healthy children (though few) have suffered immensely from this procedure.

Considering the fact that the inoculated substance is a potential toxin and foreign to the body, we need to be mindful of the possible effects of toxic impurities. Caution is advised especially with live vaccines, as the nature of microbes is to survive, regardless. (Ref. Vaccines fact or fiction? by Dr. L. D. Whyte)

THE IMMUNE SYSTEM

For vaccines to work, there has to be an adequately functioning immune system. Wouldn't it be better to help to improve the immune system, than to run the risk of challenging a possibly compromised one? The results could be devastating.

THE MILIEU IS EVERYTHING -

THE MICROBE IS NOTHING

Louis Pasteur

The immune system functions best when it is not totally preoccupied combating a plethora of infections, which we constantly encourage.

Detoxifying the body and keeping it as pure as possible, in mind, body and soul, discourages the growth of disease causing infections.

THE MILIEU IS EVERYTHING - THE MICROBE IS NOTHING

"The environment is everything, the infection is nothing", famous last words of the father of modern antibiotic therapy, Louis Pasteur. If we do not want infections to proliferate then we must clean up our internal and external environment. As stated earlier, infections will appear wherever there is tissue injury, death and decay. Anything that promotes such an environment will promote infections, example, devitalised foods, toxic chemicals and stress. Any attempt to purify ourselves by avoiding toxic impurities would result in less infection growth.

Infections are not the cause but the effect.

Once the desired environment is present, infections proliferate whether they came from outside or inside. In fact, the infections seem to benefit the body by helping to destroy and remove the toxic agent and the damaged tissues that result. This process may result in pus formation, fever, abscesses and the associated pain and discomfort. Killing of infections with antibiotics, halt the scavenging function they were performing, while leaving behind residual microbial and chemical toxins.

Natural healing tendency

The body heals itself naturally but if we continue to do the very thing, which brought on the discomfort and disease in the first place, then the healing process becomes delayed; while additional damage is being done the body. We can regain our own natural good health when we learn from the errors that resulted in disease, and stop making them.

The body will perform a series of events geared at self-purification, including elimination through body fluids, fever to denature the infections when the job is completed. (see detoxification)

What can you do?

Keeping your body pure will prevent the accumulation of toxins and the growth of infections. Fresh natural unadulterated whole foods, clean non-toxic surroundings and a mind not contaminated with toxic fear-based thoughts, will go a long way to maintain the integrity of your immune system (see sources of toxicity).

Initiate the purification (detoxification) process by using cleansers such as aloe vera, noni, castor oil, cascara, etc. Natural antibiotics like echinacea, corn silk, golden seal and garlic are extremely beneficial.

Water is essential in the dilution and removal of toxins from the body.

Meditation /relaxation. Rest is your greatest weapon. The stillness of the mind calms the turbulence of our souls. Be still and know...

'Rest is your greatest weapon'

Exercise should always be a part of this regime.

Juices the use of vegetable juices, especially, raw green juices will make the body so alkaline that the acid environment needed for microbial growth is transformed.

For more details on these topics read **...Laughter... the best medicine**

By Dr. L. Whyte

Case history

A 64 years old man, plagued with diabetes for over fifteen (15) years, developed an ulcer on his right foot. After three months of treatment, using the conventional methods of cleaning and antibiotics, there were no signs of improvement. He visited our clinic, after being told that surgical amputation was his only hope. The blood circulation was poor with a real risk of developing gangrene.

We started a treatment protocol which included detoxification, life style modification, proper nutrition, and Rife frequency treatment. The ulcer was completely healed within three weeks.

A NATURAL APPROACH TO THE MANAGEMENT OF CANCER AND OTHER IMMUNE SYSTEM DISORDERS

The body that is acidic and toxic encourages the growth of infections.

In an effort to keep these infections in check, the immune system often becomes overwhelmed and unable to cope with the emerging growth of cancer cells. These cancer cells therefore grow unchallenged. Remember that cancer and other abnormal cells may be formed from time to time without being a threat to our existence. A normally functioning immune system is quite capable of removing them.

Cancer cells are always found in an acid toxic environment, the identical condition that promotes the growth of infections.

Autoimmune disorders (diseases in which the body's immune system seem to be attacking the body's own tissues) proliferate under these same conditions. Lupus and rheumatoid arthritis are examples of autoimmune diseases.

But why should the body turn against itself? This type of behaviour suggests that the body's normal cells must have been altered. They become contaminated by the accumulated impurities and the secondary growth of infection forms, which live in or on the cells, making them appear as abnormal cells. Under these conditions the immune system, responds to protect the body and so has all rights to attack and destroy these "abnormal cells".

The method of correcting these conditions is no different from any other. The principle is the same ...... clean up the body's internal environment and the body will continue to do what it does naturally...HEAL ITSELF.

Try to understand that the body is producing new cells every second of the day. These new cells are designed to replace old damaged cells. However, if new cells were being produced in the same old acid toxic environment, then they would behave just like the old ones? Provide these cells with a cleaner, healthier environment and they will do what they do best. ...repair and replace old damaged cells.

The great miracle is not in the elimination of cancer cells, but in the body's persistence and ability to correct itself once we give it a chance. We must be prepared to change ours ways. The substitution of truth for errors in our thinking is essential in this process.

TREATMENT

The treatment of these conditions is best done with the guidance of a trained professional who is knowledgeable in the techniques of detoxification.

Cleansing herbs: such as, aloe vera, noni, sarsaparilla, and lobela.

<u>Anti-fungal and ant-oxidant</u> preparations: - e.g. pycnogenol, caprilinic acid, cat's claw, and cayenne pepper.

<u>Nutrition:</u> natural whole foods, live foods, raw foods especially vegetables.

Fasting, homoeopathic remedies, emotional release, exercise, copious water intake, guided imagery etc. are all beneficial in creating the environment that prevents the growth of cancer cells and promote healing.

BE YE TRANSFORMED BY THE RENEWING OF YOUR MIND

Romans 12:2 (kjv)

GO THY WAY AND SIN NO MORE

John 8:11 (kjv)

Case History

68 year old NH was diagnosed with cancer of the liver. On his first visit to my office, he was extremely weak and emaciated with an obvious swelling in the region of the liver. This tumour was confirmed by ultra sound studies to be eight centimetres in diameter.

His treatment involved detoxification, proper nutrition and homoeopathics.

After four months of this regime, his ultra sound report showed a normal liver. No tumour was present.

He now visits my office for social calls and informs me that he rides a bicycle five miles per day to go fishing.

Currently he has greater concerns about my health than his.

A NATURAL APPROACH TO THE MANAGEMENT OF ARTHRITIS

What is arthritis?

This is the name given to a disorder resulting in joint pains. THIS IS OFTEN ASSOCIATED WITH INFLAMMATION, SWELLING AND STIFFNESS OF THE AFFECTED JOINTS.

TYPES OF ARTHRITIS

RHEUMATOID ARTHRITIS…thought to have an autoimmune component, that is, the body's defense mechanism turning against itself.

OSTEOARTHRITIS

…degenerative changes in the joints of unknown cause thought to be due to the aging process (wear and tear).

GOUT………..a type of arthritis associated with the presence of elevated levels of uric acid in the blood.

CAUSES OF ARTHRITIS - the causes are generally said to be unknown but infections uric acid levels, autoimmune, conditions (connective tissue disorders) and trauma may be implicated

SYMPTOMS AND SIGNS... the joints often have pain, redness, swelling, stiffness, crepitations (sound and sensation of grating particles with joint movement) deformities and warmth. The conditions are often worse with initial movement from a resting position and by exposure to cold surroundings. The joint surfaces get damaged in the process and the smooth cartilaginous covering becomes eroded.

Treatment

Treatment is as far as possible dependent on the cause, so medication is given to lower the uric acid levels in gout and to kill infections where this is found (septic arthritis). For most other cases, however, the cause is unknown and hence, the treatment is predominantly designed to relieve the symptoms. Painkillers and anti-inflammatory agents are freely used and are often taken continuously to keep the pain away.

Progress and outcome

Since the real cause is not treated, it becomes necessary to take the medication continuously. Stopping the treatment therefore results in a return of the symptoms. At this point, believing that the condition is incurable, we are instructed to take the treatment for the rest of our lives.

These agents of symptom suppression are often foreign (unknown and unrecognised) by the body and because of their own acid toxic nature create an entirely new set of contaminants for the body to cope with. The ensuing responses are referred to as side effects and they lead to common problems, such as, damage to the stomach (gastritis and ulcers), liver and kidneys.

Most of these anti-inflammatory painkillers are of an acid nature. Repeated usage of such products will eventually make the body even more acidic...with disastrous results often worsening the very condition they were intended to treat.

IS THERE AN ALTERNATIVE?

Your body, which is known for its remarkable intelligence and desire to survive, has always served you well. Ask yourself… "Why would your normally intelligent body decide to punish you?" Do you have some built in code that dictates that you should have a particular malady at a specific time? Or is your body, as usual, making the best choices based on what you have given it to work with?

The older we get the greater our exposure to contaminants. The body is well aware of the danger these contaminants can do to itself, so it is always trying to purify itself of these agents. It usually employs methods of elimination such as diarrhoea, sinus, draining, cough, sweating, (associated with skin irritation, e.g. eczema, abscesses), menstrual flow, frequent urination, genital discharges etc.

We have grown to regard these methods of elimination as being bothersome and unhealthy (sickness). Without even attempting to find the reason for their appearance, we proceed to get rid of the symptoms by our most popular method …suppression.

Since the body's attempts at purifying itself are rendered unsuccessful by our intervention, then the body's next move is usually storage in safe places. This is done in order to minimize the widespread damage that free flowing contaminants may cause.

The nature of these contaminants is for the most part acidic and hence, they result in tissue damage. Damage to tissues results in cell death and decay, which encourages the growth of infections. ......resulting in further damage and toxicity. High acid levels will result in sedimentation of acid crystals.

The combined effect of acid, microbial damage and crystal formation in joints, results in the symptoms described earlier as arthritis. Any true attempt of a cure should therefore be aimed at the cause, acid toxicity based on contamination (whether self induced or from heredity).

Sources of acid contaminants

The main sources of acid contamination include

> Foods
> > Environment
> > > Thoughts

Foods are best had in their natural state (live foods), as close to the source as possible. Fresh whole foods, e.g. fruits, vegetables, ground provisions, legumes, nuts, grains are highly desirable. This considerably reduces the risk of toxicity due to preservation, adulteration or contamination.

Dead foods directly feed infections and promote acid toxicity, example, refined products like Sugar crystals, white flour, white rice, dairy products, meat, processed foods (with preservative agents, dyes, chemicals).

Environmental agents interact with our bodies and must therefore be absorbed. If the agent is acid and toxic (an impurity) then it will certainly result in tissue damage and dysfunction. (**Examples of these agents are pesticides, chemicals, smoke, radiation, cosmetics, herbicides, air fresheners, etc. It is therefore in our best interest to use safer, natural products as far as possible.**)

Mental/spiritual - The mind that is in turmoil, consumed with doubts and fears, is of necessity stressed out, anxious and tense. Such states of mind produce acid toxic changes in the physical sphere (the body). This results in acid toxic damage and subsequent tissue damage and dysfunction as mentioned earlier. Emotional conditions such as anger, hate, envy, jealousy, condemnation, judgment, unforgiveness, resentment, criticisms, shame, guilt, pride, etc. (negative emotions) are all major contributors to this process as they are all based on fear. Learning to conquer fear with love certainly helps. What we fear we cannot love and what we love we cannot fear. **Fear represents …ignorance, Love represents …knowledge.**

Learning to love and knowing oneself is the best way to master this process.

If we truly loved ourselves we would not poison, hurt or allow ourselves to be unhappy.

True healing must begin with identifying the cause and then removing toxic impurities. That is the highest priority in the process of healing. **Healing is purification and this only comes through self-adjustment.**

This may be achieved through

- physical detoxification using herbs, food, water and exercise.
- Emotional/spiritual detoxification using love.

Please refer to the chapter on detoxification for more details.

Treatment - The only true treatment is the removal of the cause through purification. Excellent adjuncts include acupuncture, homoeopathy, herbs, natural nutrition, etc. It is much better however, to take responsibility and not just take a pill.

Case History

38-year-old JC has been suffering with pain in both knees for over five years. She was diagnosed with rheumatoid arthritis and has been diligently taking medication from the start of her illness. The pains, however, persisted and some deformity of the joints were present. She consulted us, only after being told by her doctor that a surgical replacement of the knee joints was her only option.

Her treatment included detoxification, lifestyle adjustments, proper nutrition, Electro-acupuncture and herbs. Significant improvement was noted within two weeks. After four months she was totally pain-free without the use of medication.

BRONCHIAL ASTHMA

This disease is characterised by wheezing, rapid breathing and coughing, ... resulting from narrowing of the bronchi (Lung tubes). This narrowing is usually caused by spasm of the muscles, swelling of the mucosal lining, as well as secretions within the lung tubes.

Any narrowing of the lung tubes restricts the easy passage of air through the lung and also restricts the expulsion of mucus from the lungs. There is subsequently a feeling of tightness in the chest and 'air hunger'.

CAUSES

This is said to be due to an increase of sensitivity of the airways to irritants and allergens resulting in spasms and inflammation of the airways. Substances such as animal dander, dust, smoke, chemicals, environmental pollutants, and food additives have all been implicated in this condition. Anxiety, stress, exercise and infections are also contributing factors.

Who is at risk?

We all are at risk of having this condition as widespread environmental pollution as well as internal pollution persists. The condition is more often found in children under sixteen years and adults over sixty-five.

Four out of every hundred people suffer with this condition. Over the past thirty years there has been a five-fold increase in the number of cases of hospitalisation among children.

TREATMENT

Prompt medical attention can alleviate the symptoms and often prevent serious consequences.

Present medical management seeks to suppress the symptoms by using broncho-dilators, (drugs that increase the flow of air through the lung) and or reduce the level of inflammation. Neither of these methods is addressing the cause of the problem. Patients are therefore confined to a lifetime of taking one drug or the other.

IS THERE AN ALTERNATIVE?

First of all, let us understand that there is no cure unless the cause is identified.

Why should our normally intelligent body start to punish us with the discomfort of rapid breathing? Tightness of the Chest? Coughing? Air hunger? Etc.

My understanding is that it is reacting to the condition that we have imposed on it. Rapid breathing is certainly a good way to eliminate excess acid from the body. Coughing and mucous production is a way of getting rid of unwanted toxins and mucous.

How did this acid and mucous come about? ...by eating acid forming, mucous forming, constipating and dead foods.

- By exposure to environmental toxins like smoke, chemicals pesticides, etc.
- By thoughts...thoughts that are fear based, such as doubt, unbelief, hate, envy, anger, jealousy, unforgiveness, etc., thoughts of this nature are all acid forming.

The body has simply been given a toxic overload and is unable to eliminate this sufficiently by other routes, e.g. faeces. Hence, the lung is being used as an additional organ of excretion.

- What if we were to deliberately refrain from adding toxins to our bodies?
- What if we were to deliberately remove the toxins we already have?
- What are your beliefs about this condition?
- Is it incurable?
- Does it run in the family?
- Is it your unfortunate lot?

Am I a helpless victim of this condition?

I can only control the symptoms by taking medication for life

The cause is unknown

The environment is responsible

I was born with it

I am an asthmatic

- Are there any other deep-seated beliefs?
- Why do you hold this belief?

The simple response may be any of the following…

Everybody else does

The doctors say so ... and they should know.

Nobody has ever been cured of Asthma...

All my relatives have it.

This is just punishment for my sins.

People with this condition are asthmatics

"There are no pills to cure so we must endure"

Question your beliefs

Are they giving you the answers you desire?

If not ... why are you holding unto these opinions?

What if you should change these beliefs?

Remember that belief systems are only mindsets that impose limitations.

What are your fears ... what binds you to this reality?

What would happen if you faced these fears, love them and hence, begin the process of changing them?

Just for a moment, let us look at this Differently.

Suppose your symptoms are here to
help you, not to punish you?

Suppose these are attempts by the body to purify
itself of the legacy (garbage) it inherited
because of your errors?

Our detoxification program is designed to assist the body
with this process.... resulting in physical, emotional and
spiritual cleansing.

The body that is free of contaminants has no contaminants
to eliminate, therefore, no symptoms of abnormal
elimination (disease).

An error-free body is disease free.

The cleansing process can be messy ... but is necessary if
you desire the beautiful result of perfect health.

(In summary) ALTERNATIVE VIEWS ON ASTHMA

The human body is one of the most fascinating forms seen in creation. It is wonderfully made - perfect.

It has its own checks and balances.

It seems to be guided at all times by an inherent intelligence that orchestrates millions of complex functions with or without our awareness.

The body always strives to preserve itself ... maintaining good health is a part of this mandate.

I therefore find it inconceivable that this type of intelligence would suddenly turn against itself in an effort to promote self-destruction. Any such error in thinking must be due to the effect of some other intelligence (our own) interfering with the smooth running of the body's system.

The body's superior guiding intelligence, in an effort to undo the errors we have introduced, results in the inconveniences we refer to as symptoms and disease.

The lung functions as a means of air exchange, taking in needed oxygen and releasing carbon dioxide. It also uses this method to regulate the body's acid/base balance (pH) and to eliminate accumulated mucous (sputum). If one should start breathing rapidly, with lung tube constriction and inflammation (Asthma); would it be a reasonable assumption that this process of elimination is occurring because of an increased acidity and mucous accumulation? If this is so, then what are the sources of this acid and mucous? Certainly, external and internal irritants and pollutants play a significant role. We can significantly reduce our exposure to these substances by taking responsibility.

We often blame the external environment saying that individually we have no control, but do very little about the internal environment over which we have absolute control. Acid and mucous are readily introduced into our systems whenever we eat devitalised (dead) and constipating foods. These foods are also nourishing to bacteria, viruses, fungi and parasites.

Healing is a process of purification and is an entirely individual pursuit, which requires self-adjustment.

If we continue to do what we have always done we will always have what we've always had.

Treatment again has to involve detoxification and minimising the acid toxic load of the body. Cleansing herbs, chiropractic adjustments, homoeopathics, acupuncture are always helpful.

Case history

An 11 year old child has been having frequent asthma attacks from age three. He was by then quite proficient in the use of inhalers, which he had to be using daily.

His treatment under our programme, included proper nutrition, detoxification and spinal adjustment (chiropractic manipulation). He is no longer dependent on medication and gets attacks only after significant deviation from his nutritional guidelines.

NATURAL APPROACH TO THE MANAGEMENT OF HYPERTENSION

ALTERNATIVE VIEWS ON HYPERTENSION

Blood vessels (arteries and veins) are needed to transport nutrients around the body to all organ systems.

THIS IS AN ESSENTIAL FUNCTION ESPECIALLY TO VITAL AREAS LIKE THE BRAIN.

If the flow of nutrients is being restricted then the blood pressure has to increase in order to maintain adequate blood supply to the brain. Importantly, this is a reaction to a situation and not a cause in itself.

Therefore, to properly treat hypertension, we must find the reason why the blood vessels are being constricted (narrowed) and correct this.

Damage to the inside lining of the blood vessels occurs because of high levels of circulating acid toxic agents. The body then produces cholesterol-based products (atheroma) to repair the damage to the vessels. This causes narrowing of the vessels and restricted blood flow, with a subsequent increase in the blood pressure to compensate.

The conventional methods of treatment seek to use drugs to

- open up the blood vessels (vasodilators),
- slow the heart rate

- reduce fluid volume
- reduce anxiety

Such methods may reduce the blood pressure as long as the drugs are being taken, but does nothing to address the cause of the problem. Hence, the belief that the condition is incurable. But what of the side effects of these drugs? Weakness, coughing, impotence, sinus conditions, palpitations, etc. The drugs are toxic agents in their own way, adding to the original problem.

Natural approach

Getting to the source of the problem would remove the need to treat the problem. The root problem is the effect of acid toxicity on the body (contaminants, impurities).

What are the sources of acid toxicity?

Food
External causes
Mental/emotional causes

Acid and mucous are readily introduced into our systems whenever we eat devitalized (dead) and constipating foods.

These foods are also nourishing to bacteria, viruses, fungi and parasites.

Detoxification ...the only way

Acupuncture
Meditation
Herbs ...e.g. Garlic, aloe parsley
Homoeopathy
Proper nutrition

"Healing is what goes on while practitioners use clever methods to amuse patients."

voltaire

NATURAL APPROACH TO THE MANAGEMENT OF DIABETES

This is a common condition in which there is an abnormality in the regulation of sugar in the body. It is linked to an inappropriate production of insulin (the hormone used to regulate blood sugar levels). This hormone is produced in the pancreas. High or low blood levels of sugar may then result.

High levels may result in increased thickness of the blood, poor circulation, multiple system involvement, visual impairment, recurrent and chronic infections and the consequences thereof.

Cause

Generally said to be unknown but an association of heredity, obesity, and overnutrition are readily accepted.

Treatment

Standard treatment is geared to increase the amount of available insulin by either pancreatic stimulation or the direct introduction of insulin. The increased insulin levels would result in the decrease of circulating blood sugar levels. Such methods do not address the reason behind the decrease in insulin production and hence, treatment is accepted as continuous and the condition as incurable.

Side Effects

The use of these treatments, need to be closely monitored as there is a significant risk of reducing the sugar levels too low which may result in coma and even death.

Alternatives

Why is there a decrease in the body's ability to produce it's own insulin?

The malfunctioning of the pancreas may indeed be due to a genetic predisposition. However, there are many people without this family history who develop the problem and many with a significant family history that do not.

Remember that any organ system may be affected by the damage resulting from acid toxicity and subsequent microbial overgrowth within the system. If the pancreas is susceptible due to an inherent genetic weakness or otherwise, then it will certainly have its function altered by the process...hence, insulin production is affected.

When this condition persists then the pancreas loses its ability to produce insulin completely...Insulin dependent diabetes?

A conscious effort to reduce the sources of acid toxicity may yield extremely beneficial results.

This may be achieved by reducing the exposure to acid toxicity and by detoxifying the system. Refer to section on sources of acid toxicity and detoxification.

Remember that the body is always producing new cells.... but if the new cells are produced in the same old acid environment, then they must behave like the old cells. Purify the environment and the new pancreatic cells will perform their normal role by replacing old, damaged, malfunctioning ones.

Many agents are available to assist in the management of diabetes.

Natural agents like ackee, annotto, cashew bark, cerassee, can all lower the blood sugar.

Detoxification is also an essential part of this process.

Acupuncture, homoeopathy and nutrition are of utmost importance.

CASE HISTORY

C R has been on treatment for diabetes for over fifteen (15) years. Being aware of the dangers associated with this condition, he took his medication regularly; he also had frequent follow up checks with his doctor. Over the years, his medication has been gradually changed from tablets to insulin, the doses are always increasing.

Two weeks after starting our programme his dose of insulin was reduced significantly. He also reported a dramatic increase in his energy level and his general health. Two months later, his blood sugar was so well controlled in the low normal range that we had to discontinue his insulin completely.

Two years later, he is still not taking any medication yet his sugar levels remain normal. He feels wonderful, looks younger and is now enjoying life, free from the chains of medication.

HE MADE THE ADJUSTMENTS STATED EARLIER AND HE REGAINED HIS GOOD HEALTH.

HEALING IS ALWAYS WITHIN
300 YARDS OF WHERE YOU ARE
                     - ***Ancient*** Indian proverb

NATURAL APPROACH TO THE MANAGEMENT OF MENTAL DISORDERS

Mental disorders are generally considered to be outside of the ambit of natural healing methods and most practitioners would gladly refer patients so labeled, to the psychiatrist. This group of patients is considered to be of deranged behaviour and with little or no control of their affairs, mentally challenged "mad".

Widely held beliefs are

- This runs in the family
- These people are a threat to the wider society
- They are dangerous and unpredictable
- They have nothing worthwhile to contribute to society
- They are best treated by locking them up or giving them medication that keeps them subdued

Terms like schizophrenia, neurosis, panic attacks, anxiety and depression are popular labels for these persons. Once labeled, they are literally chained for life to some medication that suppresses them to an extent tolerable to those around them.

The brain is considered to be the seat of all behavioural function. What if the brain was being damaged or irritated by a toxic agent? Wouldn't the same scenario occur as in any other part of the body? High acidity, tissue injury, degeneration and secondary infection growth?

Brain function under these conditions would certainly become altered. Hence, abnormal behaviour such as poor self-control, altered memory, lack of inhibition, poor mental coordination, anti-social behaviour, pressure of thought and talk, altered reality etc. become evident.

Again detoxification and reversing the acid toxicity has met with significant success in treating these patients. Homoeopathy, herbs, nutrition and emotional release are fantastic adjuncts in the healing of these patients. Detoxification is of extreme importance and should involve mental flossing (emotional release). Homoeopathics, Bach Flower remedies, Acupuncture, Herbs and Nutrition are all important in the healing of the mental imbalance.

CASE HISTORY

This 50 year old man visited our clinic with a twenty (20) year history of manic-depressive psychosis (bipolar disorder). He had episodes of frightening mood swings, from quiet, passive suicidal depression to high energy, hyperactivity, sleeplessness, intolerable mania.

Under the guidance of his psychiatrist he was on continuous medication to "normalize" his behaviour. Once he was on his medication he remained calm and socially tolerable. Yet if ever he got off his medication his symptoms recurred. While on medication his normally brilliant intellectual abilities were severely curtailed. He was therefore chained to a lifetime of continuous medical suppression (taking medication for the rest of his life).

Within two weeks of starting our detoxification programme, he began noticing significant improvement in his general health. After four months, he was taken off all medication, his health continued to improve. Three years later, he

is still drug free with no more symptoms of this mental condition and a dramatic return to his intellectual brilliance.

His treatment protocol included detoxification, nutritional adjustment, homoeopathy, herbs and mental flossing (spiritual detoxification).

Purification through self-adjustment certainly leads to self-empowerment.

HEALING IS ABOUT PURIFICATION AND IT COMES FROM SELF-ADJUSTMENT

We have allowed ourselves to be brainwashed into thinking that health is something that we need to get from outside of ourselves, through medication, doctors, health insurers etc. Hence we engage ourselves in a frantic search for miracle cures and magic healing bullets.

Somehow we have become disconnected from the basic truth; that is for the most part, we were born perfect.

Perfect health is our divine birthright...

.......Dr. L. D. Whyte

That perfect health is the natural way of life.
That the body is always trying to heal itself
That the body does not have any pre-programming for self-destruction
That all that we need we have
That whatever we believe ...so it is (**As you believe, so it is** ...matthew 9:29 (kjv)
That we have the power to determine what we believe
That our problems are due to errors in our thinking
That our **sintoms** are due to our sins Self Inflicted Nonsense
Perfect health is our divine birthright...
... Dr. L. D. Whyte

... If we are not expressing this then we need to ask ourselves ......what have we been doing to block this normal process?

LIVE IF YOU WANT TO LIVE...Bob Marley

The choices are all up to you...if you want health then make healthy choices otherwise do whatever you please.

SOAR LIKE AN EAGLE OR SCRATCH LIKE A CHICKEN THE CHOICE IS YOURS

QUESTIONS ARE WELCOMED

CONTACT US AT:
LIFESTYLE TRANSFORMATION CENTRE AND VILLAS LTD

JAMAICA ALL NATURAL LTD
... *The healthy alternative*
JAMAICA SCHOOL OF NATURAL HEALING
NATURAL HEALING FOUNDATION
FACEBOOK..YOUR HEALTH MATTERS
E-mail: jamnatural@yahoo.com
Address...P.O BOX 673. MONTEGO BAY #2 P.O ST JAMES. JAMAICA

Jamaica
Tel. (876) 906 5683 OR..876 946 2531

www.lifestyletransformationcentre.com

PRACTICAL GUIDELINES
TO HEALTHY LIVING

Food
Best had as close to source as possible
As fresh whole foods

Exercise

Water

Meditation

ABOUT THE AUTHOR

Dr. L. D. Whyte is a registered medical practitioner. A Physician and Surgeon by training, who has dared to explore the world of complementary medicine, in an effort to provide his clients with the best possible options for their healing. He is ever willing to share the knowledge and wisdom of his experience, helping others to achieve their full potential. With the knowledge acquired, it is easy to

Recognize and remove the barriers to good health and well-being. He is of the opinion that healing starts within and therefore you are your best physician. Once you are empowered with the knowledge and truth about yourself you would enjoy healthier and more meaningful lives.

He is the Founder and Medical Director of LIFESTYLE TRANSFORMATION CENTRE AND VILLAS Ltd., a company with a mission to prevent illnesses and to promote good health naturally, through personal responsibility and self- adjustment.

Summary of Qualifications

Medical Doctor, Natural Health Consultant, Medical Microscopist, Emotional Release Therapist, Bio-Energetic Medicine, Herbology, Acupuncture, Physical Therapies, Spiritual Guidance and Counseling, Nutritional Therapist

Past President of the Association of General Practitioners of Jamaica.

Host of the radio show:Your health matters
Founding member of the Natural Healing Foundation
And Jamaica School of Natural Healing

Printed in the United States
By Bookmasters